SING CHANT LOVE

Thakur's Treasure Trove of Practical Spirituality

Shuddhaanandaa Brahmachari

LOKENATH DIVINE LIFE MISSION

KOLKATA

SING CHANT LOVE

Thakur's Treasure Trove of Practical Spirituality

(Author of Living with My Himalayan Master: Sri Sri Bhajan Brahmachari – A Biography)

Cover Design by: Sugeeti Chakraborty

Kindle formatting by: Anirban Banerjee and Sue Berg

Please send your personal experiences and comments on reading this book to susan@feelinghearts.org, and we will personally answer your email.

DEDICATION

Glory, glory, and glory to the Master!
And the boundless joy of silently
washing his holy feet
with tears of love and surrender,
and the silence that rises as a flameless flame
from the core of the being.

CONTENTS

PREFACE

The greatest joy of doing what you truly love lies in the profound experience of *non-doership*. As long as the doer is the small, fragile self—laden with conditions, fears, and preconceptions, we remain only at the surface of spiritual life. But when the sense of "I am doing" dissolves, the soul begins to taste the deeper dimensions of reality.

The spiritual journey often begins with a divine disruption—when we encounter a person or an event that pierces through the veil of ego and acquired knowledge, and awakens a long-forgotten spark of truth, selflessness, and inner divinity.

Thakur Sri Sri Bhajan Brahmachari was that one soul in my youthful years who shattered all that I thought I knew about life and its meaning. He stirred within me a silent but powerful urge to question everything—the dreams I had, the ambitions I clung to, the success I pursued—and called me, gently but insistently, to live life *from the inside out*. He challenged me to drop the facade, to listen to the quiet voice within, and to discover the infinite potential hidden in the human mind and the sacredness of this precious human body.

His mere presence made the impossible feel natural. His grace turned the pathless path into a journey of unfolding wonder. Through him, I first glimpsed the invisible hands of the *Guru*, and the quiet power of Grace that guides a soul to ask the eternal question: "**Who am I?**"

This little book is not just a memoir or a tribute. It is an invitation for you to *feel* what was real for me—a young boy with worldly dreams, who surrendered to a man who was more *presence* than person. A being who taught not through sermons, but through silence; who loved not with words, but with his whole being; who took anyone, from anywhere, into his heart—and from there, pointed them to the Divine.

I write not so that you may *know* Thakur, but that you may *feel* him. Don't try to understand him with the mind—that clever trickster that binds us to the limits of the seen and known. Rather, allow his presence to whisper into your heart. Let him be the music that moves you to sing without singing, to chant without chanting, to love without even knowing you're loving.

That is the essence of Thakur. That is the music of the soul.

Dubai 5 July 2025
Shuddhaanandaa Brahmachari

INTRODUCTION

HOW MUSIC, BHAJANS, AND KIRTANS INSPIRE SPIRITUAL LIFE

Human emotions are the very foundation of all relationships, whether with fellow beings or with the countless forms of life on this planet. It is these emotions that bind us to worldly attachments, often leading to suffering and restlessness. But this is only the beginning of the human journey.

Out of the entanglement of worldly love and transient attachments arises a subtle but persistent inner nudge—a question whispered by the soul: *"Is this all there is?"* This quiet inquiry marks the awakening of human consciousness. Throughout history, this longing for something greater has stirred the human spirit to seek higher values, deeper knowledge, and spiritual paths that transcend the visible world.

And yet, none of this seeking would be possible without the transformation of emotion—the same emotion that once clung to the transient must now rise, be purified, and redirected toward the eternal. It is this elevation of emotion, from the mundane to the sublime, that gave birth to the many spiritual paths: Jnana Yoga, the path of knowledge; Karma Yoga, the path of selfless action; Hatha Yoga, the path of discipline; and Bhakti Yoga, the path of love and surrender.

Among these, *Bhakti Yoga* has stood the test of time as a path that speaks most directly to the heart. It invites the seeker to pour out their emotions, their longings, and even their fragile ego at the feet of the Beloved—the invisible yet intimately present Divine. In this act of surrender, the false identity begins to dissolve, and the true self is slowly revealed.

Music has always played a vital role in the spiritual journey of mystics, saints, and God-intoxicated souls. Through bhajans and kirtans—devotional songs and sacred chants—these lovers of the Divine transcended their limited sense of self. As they sang, their bodies disappeared in the fire of love, and their souls danced in the light of union. Their ego melted into humility, and their hearts overflowed with love, compassion, and bliss.

In the life of **Thakur Sri Sri Bhajan Brahmachari**, this divine love expressed itself through spontaneous outpourings of song—melodies that arose not from training but from the depths of surrender. Each note was a flame of devotion, each word a sacred offering to the Divine Mother. He did not sing to perform; he sang to dissolve. He sang to unite with the Lord. And through his singing, he carried others along with him into the sacred realm of pure Being.

Today, all over the world, the path of bhajans and kirtans is blossoming again. Seekers of peace and love are gathering in temples, ashrams, homes, and open fields to sing together, calling out to the One—whether by Name or beyond all names. These devotional gatherings become rivers of divine energy, where hearts open and emotions rise like waves, offering themselves at the altar of the Infinite.

These sacred songs—whether sung in solitude or with others—begin on the physical plane but soon elevate consciousness to subtle realms. Their high vibrational frequency unlocks inner doors and awakens the dormant divine presence within. What begins as chanting becomes meditation, and meditation becomes absorption. And in that absorption, the seeker merges with the Beloved in an ecstasy beyond words, a bliss beyond form—a state we know as *Samadhi*, *Moksha*, *Nirvana*.

In this small booklet, you will discover the essence of that inner singer, that hidden lover of the Divine, waiting to awaken through the life, songs, and teachings of this Himalayan sage—Thakur Bhajan Brahmachari. His entire life was a song, a living bhajan, a ceaseless offering in the sacred fire of divine love.

Bhajans and kirtans remain the most accessible doorway to spiritual union. Even for those unfamiliar with practices or scriptures, a single heartfelt chant can open the floodgates of grace. In singing, you are not just invoking the Divine—you are being drawn into the embrace of the One who has always been waiting for you in your own heart, with arms wide open and love beyond measure.

This—this sacred union—is the true purpose of human life.

WHO IS THAKUR?

CHAPTER 1

THAKUR'S NAME AS BHAJAN, AND HIS NATURAL GIFT OF SONG

When Thakur Sri Sri Bhajan Brahmachari was still a young boy, he fell seriously ill, so gravely that death seemed near. At that critical time, an old, saintly woman named Bhairavi Ma visited and offered him a cure. After restoring the child's health, she turned to his mother, Ma Priyabala, and said:

"From now on, call this child Hari Bhajan—the divine chant of God. One day, his voice will awaken devotion in the hearts of countless people. His songs will be filled with the sacred vibrations of divine love, and all who hear them will be drawn to the path of God. When the time comes, he will leave home to serve the larger family of the Lord. Do not hold him back then."

Not long after this, one day Ma Priyabala went to the nearby temple of Lakshmi-Narayana, taking young Bhajan along with her. She asked him to wait outside while she went into the sanctum to offer her prayers. When she returned, she found her son missing. Alarmed, she searched the temple grounds until—under a sprawling banyan tree—she discovered her little Bhajan sitting cross-legged, singing bhajans in deep devotion to Mother Kali.

She stood still, astonished. No one had ever taught him these chants, yet here he was, singing with such feeling, such depth, and such ease—his voice flowing like a river of devotion. It was as if the Divine Mother Herself was singing through him.

During their time in Calcutta, whenever Bhajan visited the temple of Mother Kali at Kalighat with his mother, he would sit quietly among the sadhus, listening with rapt attention as they sang to the Divine Mother. Without anyone asking, he would join in. At home, he would hum these songs to himself, and his notebooks were filled with sketches and drawings of Mother Kali. Devotion had taken root in his heart from the earliest age.

Music became his world. It was the one thing that fully captivated his attention. He adored those who sang devotional songs and felt a deep spiritual pull toward them. Whenever he heard bhajans, he would slip into a kind of quiet ecstasy. No one taught him how to sing—songs simply poured out of him, flowing from the heart with innocence and love. His was a natural gift, and his voice carried a divine fragrance. Those who heard him sing were effortlessly transported into the presence of the Divine.

The young Bhajan's devotional singing became a spiritual event in itself. People came in large numbers just to listen. His voice was awakening something sacred in the hearts of all who heard him. Even as a child, he was already guiding souls toward devotion and love.

As he grew older, his presence and his voice only deepened in power and grace. He was often invited to religious gatherings to sing bhajans, and wherever he went, people flocked to listen. His songs were not mere melodies; they were living prayers. Listeners found an instant connection—not just with the singer, but with the divine Reality behind the song.

The first time I met him and heard him sing, I was utterly transported. It was as if the boundaries of the world had dissolved. I could not relate that moment to anything else in my life. He was not merely singing—he was invoking the Lord into the very space we were in. It felt as though we were sitting in the actual presence of the Supreme Being.

What moved me most was witnessing him enter into *bhav-samadhi*—a state of divine rapture that came slowly, as his eyes closed and his voice deepened. This was the same state often seen in Sri Ramakrishna, where the soul, overwhelmed with love for the Divine, merges into blissful silence.

Thakur used his singing not just as an offering of love, but as a way to teach. Through his songs, he conveyed his spiritual teachings—simple, profound truths about the path of devotion, the grace of the Guru, and the importance of spiritual practice. He did not give formal lectures. He did not need to. His presence was his message. His life was his teaching.

To those weary from the struggles of life, yearning for a little peace, his songs were like the first rain on parched earth. The divine chants that flowed from him opened hearts, stirred dormant devotion, and lit the inner lamp of longing for God.

Truly, he lived his name—*Bhajan*—and he became, for countless souls, the divine song that called them home.

CHAPTER 2

THAKUR, THE EPITOME OF POSITIVE POWER

An enlightened Master is living proof that we, too, can attain the highest state of God-realization. While ordinary mortals remain entangled in worldly cravings and are helpless before the power of Maya, the divine play of illusion and ignorance, the truly awakened perceive the futility of chasing happiness through material means. Such souls choose to walk the sacred path shown by great Masters and, in time, awaken to the light of Truth.

Thakur once said, *"It is not true that in Kali Yuga it is difficult to attain liberation. It is just the opposite. In previous Yugas, tremendous austerities were required to be free. But now, if you trust your Guru and patiently persevere with mantra Japa (Naam Smarana), you can attain God-realization quickly."*

These words, radiant with divine optimism, come directly from the heart of an enlightened Master. Contrary to what many believe—that in these troubled times, when negativity saturates the atmosphere, spiritual practices are slow to bear fruit—Thakur emphatically asserts that this is in fact the most opportune time. One need not perform harsh penance. Instead, offer your heart to the Divine, fill it with the sacred vibration of the Guru Mantra, and surrender like a child at the feet of the Cosmic Mother. The Mother, or the Universe itself, is ever awake, ever ready to support and uplift those who walk the path of spiritual seeking—no matter how steep or uncertain it may seem.

Mantra, Guru, and Grace—these are not separate. They arise from the same quantum ground of pristine reality. Together, they work in harmony to guide the seeker from darkness to light, from bondage to liberation.

To me, Thakur is the very embodiment of divine positivity. His words carry the weight of truth and the warmth of infinite assurance. If one can simply believe in his words and follow them sincerely, a profound transformation is inevitable.

CHAPTER 3

IN HIS PRESENCE, ONE FELT GOD

Thakur lived a normal, unpretentious, and natural life. He was not someone who constantly spoke of God, spirituality, or scriptural disciplines. Many who came close to him, especially those expecting a conventional holy man, often misunderstood this simplicity.

In India, it is generally expected that monks and saints, when surrounded by devotees, would speak only about divine knowledge, scriptural wisdom, and spiritual practices. But **Thakur was a living sage**. His presence alone communicated everything one needed to know about **God and Godliness**.

People would arrive and instantly feel drawn to him, as iron filings are drawn to a magnet. Even when he spoke of mundane or routine aspects of life, his words carried an **unmistakable vibration of peace**—a kind of happiness one could not find anywhere else. Often, his ordinary conversations delivered extraordinary insights, and the gathered devotees would sit spellbound, unwilling to leave. **His very presence was a greater teaching than any words could offer.**

Those of us who were close to him would feel completely empty when he was away. He was **pure love**. His presence was **living wisdom**. He was **divine love in action**.

Thakur lived in total **simplicity and humility**, yet his spiritual presence cast such a magical aura that even a brief meeting with him left a lasting impression. He was the **embodiment of joy and bliss**, inspiring all to judge less, introspect more, and walk the inner path of **peace and happiness**.

Oh! What golden days they were—when we sat at the **feet of God walking the earth**. All glory to the **Master of Love**, who lived only to give joy.

CHAPTER 4

THAKUR, THE PLAYFUL CHILD

Thakur was the most playful soul I have ever encountered. Though he was my Master, he often made me feel as if he were my dearest friend—we played pranks on each other, laughing like children in a boundless field of joy.

During festive occasions, the ashram would transform into a grand spiritual celebration, drawing devotees from far and wide. Holi was one such festival, and on that day, Thakur would become like the playful Krishna—his joy infectious, his spirit radiant. With vibrant colors in hand, he would color not only our clothes but our hearts. To the unknowing eye, it was merriment; but to those who looked deeper, his every gesture—his touch, his smile, his playful smearing of colors, and the colors offered reverently at his feet—was a divine message: that at the core of every human being lies a longing to love and to be loved in the purest, most innocent way.

He would often say: "*When you fall in love with Krishna, like the Gopis of Brindavan, your physical cravings dissolve. What binds you to the body fades, and for the first time, you experience a feeling so natural, so sacred, so utterly enchanting—it intoxicates you.*"

To be in the presence of a living, enlightened Master during his time on Earth is one of the rarest blessings the universe can bestow. I never saw him formally teach, preach, or even engage in structured yoga or meditation. He simply lived—moment to moment—in the spontaneous, unfiltered joy of an innocent child. And yet, one part of him was deeply rooted in the world, while the other remained ever immersed in supreme consciousness.

He was a Presence beyond words.

CHAPTER 5

THAKUR WAS MORE MOTHER THAN FATHER

To me, **Thakur was more a mother than a father**. In his physical presence, anyone who had the good fortune of spending time with him felt an overwhelming sense of motherly love and unconditional forgiveness. He was too gentle to reprimand his disciples or devotees, even when they erred. I often saw how some took advantage of his motherly softness. Yet, his compassion was boundless. His healing energy worked miracles, *as naturally as fragrance belongs to flowers.*

This is just as true today. **Pray for his grace now, and he is with you—Here and Now.**

As *Antaryamin*, the Inner Knower, he knew everything, but chose to remain soft like a mother rather than stern like a father. On **Guru Purnima**, we would worship him as the **Divine Mother**, and in those moments, we clearly saw the Mother's presence in him. He spoke in the hearts of the sincere as the **voice of conscience**. The truly blessed heard and followed his subtle guidance. Others, content to remain at the surface, were simply happy seeing his external form and expected miracles in their lives.

CHAPTER 6

THAKUR, THE COMPASSIONATE LISTENER

Q: Why did Thakur spend so much time talking to people about the mundane things of life?

Thakur had a deep love for all householder devotees. He welcomed them warmly and listened attentively as they poured out their hearts, sharing the struggles and confusions of their daily lives. He often said, *"If I only talk about God and the higher truths, people will lose interest. Their minds are burdened with worldly worries. First, I must meet them where they are."*

Thakur understood that most people live entangled in repetitive, unresolved issues, unsure of how to navigate life's emotional storms. So, he came down from the sublime heights of *Samadhi* to this worldly plane—not to discuss the trivial, but to gently lift the weary minds of devotees from the mundane to the sacred.

Through compassionate listening, he offered a subtle teaching—how to truly listen with love. Not to speak over others, but to hear them fully, as an act of presence and care.

In this way, Thakur helped even the most ordinary individuals begin a journey of *self-purification*, guiding them with simple yet powerful practices like *mantra Japa* and surrender to the Supreme Will. His presence itself was transformative, showing how the divine can dwell even in the small, often overlooked corners of daily life.

CHAPTER 7

THAKUR'S PRESENCE BEYOND THE PHYSICAL

Q: Thakur, your disciples and devotees are spread across the world. Many of them cannot come to you in person to seek guidance, and yet I see they often find solutions to their problems just by praying to you. How is this possible?

Thakur: "*Though they are not physically with me, they have my picture on their altars at home. When they pray with tears of devotion and seek my help, I can hear them. By divine grace, their prayers are answered, and their life obstacles are removed.*"

Enlightened Masters, out of deep compassion, descend from the heights of supreme consciousness to the earthly realm—not for themselves, but for others. While they dwell among us, they bring with them the light of divine awareness and the grace to heal, uplift, and transform.

How else would the common man, lost in ignorance and attachments, ever comprehend the mystery of divine intelligence that sustains all creation?

Sages like Thakur have no desires left for themselves—their ego has been transformed into divine Self. Their sole purpose is to love, serve, and spread compassion. They become radiant beacons of divine love, forgiveness, and healing, helping others awaken to the true purpose of human life.

Human beings cannot see God directly, but from time immemorial, they have encountered divinity in human form, in the living Buddhas who walk among us. These self-realized masters are living reminders of *Dharma*, the eternal law that governs the universe.

Thakur reveals a beautiful truth: even if a devotee prays sincerely before his picture, he can hear it. His grace, invoked by devotion, can uplift the seeker and remove all obstacles—bringing healing, peace, and prosperity.

FINDING GURU

CHAPTER 8

THE GURU APPEARS IN YOUR LIFE

In the Vedic tradition, the *Guru* is revered as the one who embodies divine qualities in human form for the seeker. Sadly, the term is often misused today to refer to those with mere worldly skills or superficial mastery of mundane subjects.

A true Guru lives the highest wisdom—wisdom accessible only to one who has attained a deeply evolved state of body-mind perfection.

Thakur Sri Sri Bhajan Baba was often asked when and how one finds a Guru to guide them on the spiritual path. In his simple and profound way, he would say:

"Just as the honeybee comes naturally when the flower blossoms, so too, when a deep yearning awakens in your heart to know the secret of peace and happiness, the Guru appears in your life. Either you go to your beloved Master, or the Master comes to you."

Once the Guru enters your life, if you are a sincere seeker, you will begin to notice inner transformation:

Your ingrained patterns that once caused stress and tension start to shift.

Your attitude towards those who hurt you begins to soften.

And your entire perception of life undergoes a subtle yet powerful change.

All of this unfolds from within, through a natural interplay of *sadhana* (spiritual practice) and the Guru's grace.

"Bin Guru Gyan Nehi" - Without the Guru, true wisdom is not possible.

The Guru can guide you—if you are willing to help yourself by quietly and faithfully following his instructions.

Guru and his instructions are one and the same.

CHAPTER 9

THE DIFFERENCE BETWEEN GURU AND GOD

Q: Thakur, many times, we get confused between the Guru and God. Why does this happen, and how can we overcome such doubts and distrust?

Thakur: "*When you work with a living teacher, it's very different from worshipping a picture or idol of God in a temple or on your home altar. The human mind finds it difficult to perceive a fellow human being as being as supreme as God. Yet, you often hear that unless one sees the Guru as God, the true transmission of the Guru's grace cannot take place.*"

In day-to-day life, it's not easy to hold the same feeling for your Guru as you do for God. This is the root of your confusion. True surrender to the Guru happens not when you worship his personality, but when you realize that it is the Presence of the

Guru in your life that allows the seed of divinity within you to blossom.

Even if you live with a realized Master, there is no guarantee of your enlightenment. Everything depends on the depth and intensity of your yearning to manifest the divinity that already resides within you.

The more sincerely you follow the personal guidance of your Master, and the more selflessly you serve (Guru-seva) without expectation, the sooner you will begin to experience the true power of the Guru and the blessings that flow from that connection.

Almost everyone on this path faces this confusion at first. But those who rise above it are the ones who do not wallow in guilt. Instead, they apply themselves diligently to daily meditation and prayer. Over time, they begin to feel a deep and unshakable connection to the living Presence of the Guru, and joyfully walk the path, holding his grace as the only true reality—the force behind all inner transformation.

Lage raho bhai, bonat banat ban jai — Keep persevering on your spiritual path with devotion and love for your teacher, and more importantly, for his teachings. In time, you will attain moksha—liberation from all suffering.

CHAPTER 10

THE IMPORTANCE OF GURU BHAKTI

Thakur often reminded us, "*Householders need not perform severe austerities to attain God.*" He would say, "*If you have a deep yearning for God and can place complete trust in your Guru—if you can follow his guidance without doubt—you will progress swiftly on the spiritual path. You will begin to experience how your Guru is always protecting you, how deeply he loves and cares for you. The more you realize this truth, the deeper your Guru Bhakti will grow, and the closer you will move towards God-realization.*"

Gurudev emphasized that the path of surrender and love is time-tested, accessible, and appropriate for most people. The more rigorous paths—like Hatha Yoga or Jnana Yoga—are suitable only for those who can discipline themselves under the guidance of a true adept. But *true devotion to your Guru or your Ishta Devata can never go in vain.* When the time is ripe, such devotion draws down a flood of divine grace. This path of love and surrender is anchored in patience, humility, and perseverance. Guru's Grace, Gurudev affirmed, constantly surrounds the sincere disciple, even when unseen.

In the end, it is always the Guru who leads us to our Ishta—the Chosen Form of God. He is the bridge. He holds the rudder of our boat of life, guiding us toward the other shore where freedom from pain and suffering awaits. That is *Guru-Dham*—the divine kingdom where God alone reigns, where all conflict dissolves into peace and harmony.

And when you begin to breathe consciously, you will feel the universe breathing through you. You will sense that this vast, breathing cosmos is but the expanded presence of your Guru. Feel every breath as your Guru breathing in and out, keeping you alive for the sacred purpose of realizing God.

CHAPTER 11

THE POWER OF SURRENDER

Q: Those who completely depend on you and surrender to you, seeing you as God—do you take full responsibility for them?

Thakur: "*To surrender totally to the Guru is not easy for householders. It is a rare and exalted state of mind, possible only when one's inner being is purified in the fire of deep longing for the Divine and for the Guru. However, you can begin by maintaining regular contact with your Guru, by serving him with love and humility, by listening attentively to his words, and sincerely trying to implement them in your daily life.*"

The Guru always knows which student is sincerely striving to follow the teachings and is focused on embodying love and compassion in action. Grace flows naturally toward such a student. Genuine seekers do not limit the Guru to his physical form, nor do they seek to impress him with superficial acts of devotion.

They know the Guru is *Antaryamin*—the indwelling witness who perceives every thought. There can be no deception before such divine presence. Even the little that a sincere disciple practices becomes the means for drawing nearer to the Light that the Guru kindles within the heart.

The more sincerely you assume the responsibility of being a true disciple—walking the discipline laid down by the Master—the more you will find the Master guiding you, both inwardly and outwardly, at every step. Such disciples blossom naturally, gracefully.

CHAPTER 12

HOW CAN I SEE GOD?

Q: A devotee once asked Thakur: "Why don't we see God, even though we do our Japa every day?"

Thakur replied: *"Do you know how much intense sadhana I myself had to undertake in the Himalayas and at Vrindavan? To truly see God, you must reach a stage where nothing else matters—where your heart cries out for God every moment, where you feel you cannot even live without the Divine presence. When your entire being yearns only for God, and all desires fall away, then the ego dissolves, and God-realization dawns.*

But right now, you still want worldly pleasures—samsarik sukh—and alongside that, you carry a faint wish to see God! Do you truly think you are ready for God-realization?"

Thakur's words are not a rebuke, but a call to honesty and depth. Many seekers unknowingly equate God-realization with worldly accomplishments—something to be achieved with a bit of effort and the right technique, like mastering a skill. But God is not an object. God is not separate from us.

Most of us grow up with an image or idea of God—something inherited from parents, culture, or religion. These impressions form a concept of a God "out there," rather than the living Presence "in here." Real sadhana begins when this borrowed idea starts to fall apart.

This is where the role of the **Guru** becomes pivotal. The Guru is not merely a giver of knowledge, nor someone to feed our curiosity. He works both **outside and within**—to awaken, challenge, pull, and push the seeker through the many layers of consciousness. Rather than giving answers, he creates situations that force the seeker to confront life, to unlearn conditioned beliefs, and to shed the mind's deeply ingrained habits.

The Guru doesn't decorate the ego with more information. He purifies the very root of ignorance by making the seeker *live* the truth, not just *know* it intellectually.

So, when Thakur asks, *"Do you really think you are ready for God-realization?"*—he's inviting deep introspection. Many enter the path of spirit due to curiosity, suffering, or a moment of grace. But the path is not for the curious alone; it is for the courageous.

Even the slightest blemish in the mind—the residue of past impressions, desires, fears, and ambitions—can obstruct the flowering of the Ultimate. To be ready for that divine blossoming, one must become empty, free of all samskaras (mental impressions), and utterly present.

Only then does the great alchemy occur—when the seeker, the seeking, and the sought dissolve into **One**.

The knower, the known, and the knowing become one undivided consciousness.

In that moment, **God-realization and Self-realization are revealed to be One.**

CHAPTER 13
ON MAYA AND GURU'S GRACE

Devotee: What is Maya?

Thakur: "*Maya is your deep attachment and attraction to the transient—worldly people and things.*"

D: Why do we fall into its trap?

T: "*Because it is the natural law of this worldly life.*"

D: Isn't it true that Guru Shakti is stronger than Maya Shakti?

T: "*Yes, that is true. But the Guru never violates the divine laws that govern this world of Maya.*"

D: Then, can we overcome Maya with Guru Kripa?

T: "*Yes, but it requires intense sadhana in daily life. You must anchor yourself in constant remembrance of the Divine Name or Guru Mantra. Engage with the world in a state of mindful awareness—be* *loving and compassionate, bring joy to others. Do not let your ego react simply because someone failed to respect you.*

Freedom from Maya comes through genuine love and surrender to the Guru. The Guru does not meddle with karmic law but works silently—both within and without—to dispel the darkness of ignorance and lift the disciple into intuitive knowledge of the Divine.

The word Guru in Sanskrit means 'the dispeller of darkness.' And so, he is."

Let us remember that true Guru Bhakti is not sentimental attachment or outward ritual, but the quiet fire of surrender, service, and self-purification. When practiced with sincerity, it becomes the most natural and joyful path to Divine Union.

CHAPTER 14

THE GREATEST MIRACLE IS YOUR OWN TRANSFORMATION

Q: Thakur, what about those who display all kinds of vibhuti and miracles and attract large followings? Are they leading people to the true path of God?

Thakur: "*No, that is not the right path. True transformation does not come by drawing people through displays of supernatural powers or siddhis. In fact, it causes more harm than good. Once the followers witness miracles, they begin to expect more miracles. Their attention shifts from spiritual practice to the spectacle. Their faith becomes dependent on the next magical display, and the deeper purpose of spiritual evolution is lost.*"

These words are filled with wisdom. I have seen this in real life—many followers, enchanted by their Guru's miraculous powers, end up remaining on the surface of spiritual life. They miss the depth they came seeking. Thakur is right—it does more harm than good. One may argue that such miracles help generate faith, but in truth, they often distract. The seekers begin to glorify the 'godman', while continuing to live in their own inner darkness.

Yes, great sages may manifest miracles. I have witnessed this in my own Gurudev. But their miracles were never for show. They flowed spontaneously from pure compassion, from a place of utter selflessness and divine love.

In this sacred path of spirituality, never forget: **the greatest miracle is your own transformation.** It is your sincerity, your trust, your devotion, and your surrender that lead you to the real miracle—**Self-realization.**

Let this be your reminder: **Choose love over fear, discernment over haste, and practice over spectacle.** The path may be slow and silent, but it leads to the boundless ocean of **Paramananda**—the bliss of Divine union.

ON LIVING LIFE

CHAPTER 15

PAIN AND AGONY ARE INEVITABLE IN LIFE

Q: Thakur, why must we go through so much pain and agony in life to progress on the spiritual path?

Thakur: "*It is only through pain and suffering that a person is drawn closer to God. It is through these moments of deep anguish that one begins to realize how fleeting and hollow worldly pleasures truly are. When you see that material desires cannot bring lasting peace, only then do you turn towards the Divine for refuge. And when you begin to follow the guidance of saints, sages, and your Guru, you start to feel God's protection and love surrounding you. Even amidst your suffering, you come to know: God is your own. In times of pleasure and worldly happiness, you tend to forget Him.*"

Thakur's words awaken us to a deeper truth—that we must become more aware of the subtle outcomes of both pain and pleasure. The cycle of joy and sorrow is not a random occurrence, but the very structure of human life—a divine design meant to keep us seeking, searching, and questioning.

Though we often name our quest as a pursuit of happiness or success, history has shown that such pursuits alone cannot satisfy the soul. It is this constant seeking that binds us—to desires, to attachments, to expectations—and eventually entangles us in suffering. From the peak of success, we may fall into the valley of failure; from moments of pleasure, we slide into the shadows of pain. And beneath these surface experiences lie the deeper anxieties and fears we unconsciously create.

Yet these very stumbles are not without grace. Each fall carries the hidden gift of humility. Each struggle makes us more compassionate. Suffering grounds us—it anchors us to our inner world and invites us to turn inward, toward silence, contemplation, and meditation. It becomes the sacred journey from darkness to light.

If life offered only pleasure, comfort, and praise, how would the soul ever be refined? Just as gold must endure fire to be purified, the human spirit is refined through adversity. As Thakur says, in times of ease and joy, we often forget the Divine and the infinite grace that sustains us.

Let pain remind you not of despair, but of the presence of God, waiting to be discovered within.

CHAPTER 16

ON EXPECTATIONS AND PERFECTION

Thakur would often say: "*You will never find anyone who perfectly matches your expectations. And even if you do, it will not last. But if you raise yourself, you will fulfill your own expectations and find happiness.*"

Other than the Supreme Divine—the pure awareness that is beyond time and form—what or who can truly be perfect? Only God is perfect, for He is without beginning or end. Everything else is marked by imperfection, bound by birth and death.

Once we realize this fundamental truth—that perfection is a myth in the realm of duality—we let go of the illusion of expecting others to be ideal. We begin to live more authentically, without masks or pretenses.

Thakur's insight goes deeper. He invites us not to chase perfection in others, but to focus on continual self-upgradation.

Through meditation, mindful living, and dedicated effort, we raise our own vibration and energy. We may not become perfect, but we grow—our awareness expands, and our presence begins to radiate peace.

As our frequency rises, we attract harmony, success, and goodness—not only for ourselves, but for those around us.

CHAPTER 17

SIMPLICITY, SPEECH, AND KARMA

Thakur lived with great simplicity and urged others to do the same. He would ask: "*The time you take to say a few kind and healing words is the same time you take to utter words that hurt and humiliate another. Why waste your breath creating bad karma through anger and cruelty? Don't forget—whatever you give out today, you will receive in return, sooner or later!*"

These are golden words, to be engraved in our hearts—not just intellectually understood but internalized through constant reflection and practice.

Peace begins within. When we learn to calm our own minds, we stop hurting others. We begin to view the world through the lens of compassion and humility.

There are no coincidences in life. Every hardship, every storm we face, often has its roots in unconscious actions and words—hurts we may have inflicted, knowingly or unknowingly. Karma does not discriminate. Like the law of gravity, it operates whether or not we believe in it.

Thakur gently reminds us: what we send out into the universe—good or bad—returns to us. Let us then choose words that heal, acts that uplift, and a life that sows peace in every direction.

CHAPTER 18

THE DILEMMA OF WHO TO TRUST

Q: Thakur, is trusting a person and trusting God the same?

Thakur: "*Faith and trust are indeed the same in essence. But when it comes to trusting a person, it must be done with careful judgment and a sense of caution. It should never be done in haste. However, when you love or trust God, it must be without judgment, unconditionally. You must know that God's love for you is boundless and without condition. There should be no trace of doubt when you place your trust in God.*"

Thakur is guiding us toward a vital aspect of *sadhana*—to be mindful and discerning about where we invest our emotions. When we place trust in a person, we must remain alert so that we are not left vulnerable or misled. You may have noticed in your own life how deeply your emotional state is affected by those whom you love or are closely attached to. At your workplace, though you interact with many people, your emotional entanglement is minimal, and even if things go wrong, they don't often disturb you deeply. But in your home, your close relationships often hold a mirror to your heart. Their words or actions can stir your emotions, sometimes leading to immense stress or anxiety.

That is why Thakur's words are profoundly practical—invest your emotions wisely. Misplaced trust in the wrong person can lead to prolonged and repeated suffering.

But **God-love** is of a different nature. It is rooted in surrender, nurtured through *Japa*, *Dhyana*, and silent remembrance. It is free of expectations. It grows slowly, steadily, and purely.

Thakur was a living sage. His very presence expressed the essence of God and Godliness. For those who were close to him, even his absence felt like an unbearable emptiness. He was the embodiment of pure love.

CHAPTER 19

SHOULD WE GET INVOLVED IN OTHERS' SUFFERINGS?

Q: Thakur, in our society we see so much injustice and cruelty. Should we just live a pious life and ignore what happens to others? If all injustice is happening by the will of God, then why should we get involved and suffer for the sake of others?

Thakur: *"If someone insults your mother, or abuses your wife and children in front of your eyes, would you be able to tolerate that? Could you remain indifferent? If you are ready to fight for justice when it concerns your own family, then why remain silent when others in society suffer the same injustice? How can you stay unmoved, without protest? No—never stay silent in the face of injustice and cruelty. You must raise your voice and take action to stop it."*

"You must always stand against injustice. Those who do not are not worthy of being called human!"

Thakur's words are deeply practical and illuminating. We are quick to rise in defense of our own family members, but when others suffer, we suddenly invoke spirituality and forgiveness to justify our inaction. According to Thakur, this is not true spirituality—it is selfishness and a shallow awareness of our higher calling as just and compassionate human beings.

If everyone limits their spiritual concern only to their own kin, we create a society barren of true spiritual values, void of mutual respect, cooperation, and the collective spirit of well-being. True spirituality upholds the Vedic ideal of "*Sarve bhavantu sukhinah*"—"May all be happy, may all be free of suffering." It sees the Divine in every being and calls upon us to build a world founded on justice, support, and dignity for all.

Thakur does not advocate violence; he calls for *non-violence rooted in courageous compassion*—a non-violence that defends the vulnerable and ensures that society is just, peaceful, and inclusive.

CHAPTER 20

ASHRAM POLITICS, POWER STRUGGLES, CORRUPTION

Q: A devotee asks Thakur: "You speak of establishing Ashrams and Maths as sacred spaces, but often they become entangled in politics, power struggles, money, and corruption. Why does this happen?"

Thakur: *"This is how human nature expresses itself, especially in the influence of Kali Yuga. Just as Ashrams are meant to carry sacredness, the dominating energies of this age bring with them distortion. You cannot expect people to behave like they would in Satya Yuga while living in Kali Yuga. When the time is right, God Himself will transform the influence of this Yuga and bring about a shift in human consciousness. All of it is His divine play—the powerful influence of Time (Yuga) at work!"*

Such words bear the ring of prophetic truth. Thakur deeply believed in the vision of Ashrams as sanctuaries of inner renewal—places where the soul could return again and again to awaken its innate longing for divine joy. Yet even he was not untouched by the disillusionment that came when ego, ambition, and rivalry crept into these sacred spaces.

He would often express his pain, saying, *"I created this place as a haven for weary souls—a space of rest, reflection, and the loving guidance of a living teacher. A place not just for learning, but also for unlearning—so the mind may become a gentler place to live."*

Thakur emphasized the nature of **Kali Yuga**—an age marked by conflict, chaos, and spiritual confusion. In this time, those who sincerely long for truth, moral clarity, and inner purity are often tested more severely. The world, driven by surface values and material cravings, may appear to favor those attached to flesh and form. And yet, this too shall pass.

The ancient Vedic wisdom teaches that Time is cyclical. After darkness comes light, after descent, ascent. Evil may triumph temporarily, but it is always Truth that triumphs in the end.

Thakur reminds us: God's will is supreme. Our path is to align with that universal will, to rediscover our essential nature—pure existence, consciousness, and bliss (Sat-Chit-Ananda). Let us not be discouraged by what we see around us, for everything is unfolding under the watchful eye of the Divine.

CHAPTER 21

WHAT IS MINE AND WHAT IS GOD'S

Q: Thakur, I feel that whatever is in my control belongs to me. But do I still have to say everything belongs to God?

Thakur: "*Yes, you must reflect deeply on what truly belongs to you. Even if you claim something is yours, does that make it so? Think of your dearest ones—your mother, your father—were you able to stop them from leaving you at the time of death? Then what right do you have to claim ownership? What control do you really have? Everything belongs to Him.*"

The fundamental error of human beings lies in ignorance of the question, "*Who am I?*" In this ignorance, we mistake names and forms for reality. Look at your own body: a vast, intricate community of trillions of cells, functioning with extraordinary intelligence—yet are *you* the one making your heart beat or your liver function?

You don't own your organs, nor do you run them consciously—life sustains you through a deeper force, *Prana* or life-energy, the divine principle that animates all existence.

So, what is truly yours?

Even those you call your "own" can depart suddenly. Can you stop that? When illness or death arrives unannounced, and no money or medicine can help, who decides what happens next?

True spirituality arises from this deep inner inquiry. It's not just about intellectually understanding what is yours and what is not, but about going to the core of your being—to see the ego for what it is and awaken to the higher Self. That alone can resolve the illusions of ownership and control and open the path to inner freedom.

CHAPTER 22

YOU MAY FAIL, BUT GURU AND GOD NEVER FAIL

Q: Thakur, there are times when we are confronted with threats and suffering from all sides. What do you expect us to do at such times?

Thakur: *"You may fail, but your Guru and God will never fail. Know that when life places you in situations beyond your control, when you feel surrounded and helpless, that is the true moment to test your trust and patience in your Guru and God. Ask yourself: Are you worrying more, or are you doing Japa with full surrender? What are you really doing? Are you caught in fear and anxiety, or do you hear the quiet voice within saying, 'Thakur is here—why worry?' A true devotee is never destroyed. God protects those who surrender to Him. Trust, and be without fear."*

These are not mere words of consolation; they are words of *eternal assurance* spoken by one who is rooted in the supreme consciousness. Thakur is not trying to soothe us superficially—he is presenting a profound truth. Difficult times are not just phases to endure, but moments to reflect deeply: How strong is your trust? How sincere is your surrender?

When life is stable and smooth, faith goes unquestioned. But in times of extreme adversity, the ego, fear, and doubt rise to the surface. Thakur brings a higher perspective to these moments: if you can increase your mantra *Japa*, your prayer, and your surrender in such times, then not only do you begin to feel divine grace, but your faith deepens. That, he says, is *true spiritual progress*—not escape from suffering, but inner transformation through it.

CHAPTER 23

HOW THE GURU MANTRA SILENCES THE CHATTER OF THE MIND

Why did Thakur place such emphasis on *Japa* as a path to liberation? He would often tell his devotees:

"With devotion, keep repeating your Guru Mantra and observe your thoughts. Gradually, you will begin to feel the Guru's grace and learn to live without anger and anxiety."

All our suffering—fear, anxiety, restlessness—originates in the mind. These patterns of thought are deeply ingrained, often operating automatically and unconsciously. Unless we interrupt this cycle, the mind continues generating low-vibration thoughts that attract corresponding negative circumstances, energies, and people.

But Thakur, echoing the wisdom of the *Gita*, shows us a way out: *"Urdharet Atmana Atmanam"*— "Uplift the self by the Self." He teaches us to uplift the mind with the help of our own higher mind through the power of mantra. Chanting the Guru Mantra consistently begins to shift the vibrational field of the mind. Over time, this sacred repetition creates a shield—an energy field of higher consciousness that lower vibrations cannot penetrate.

If we allow the mind to remain a slave to its conditioned patterns, even wealth and success cannot bring lasting happiness. But when a sincere seeker puts faith in the words of the Guru and takes up the practice of *Japa* with love and sincerity, the results are profound.

Repeated chanting of the mantra forms new neurological pathways in the brain. It evokes the release of "happy hormones," and activates centers in the brain associated with love, compassion, and spiritual joy. This is not just mystical philosophy; it is spiritual science.

This is what Thakur emphasized tirelessly: Trust your Guru's words. Begin your practice—even if your mind resists at first. Commit to it with intention, without craving instant results. Let your heart do the work.

In time, this very practice draws in the miraculous power of Grace. The Guru's presence begins to shine from within, and the seeker is lifted beyond the bondage of mind, into the realm of spiritual freedom and liberation.

THE PATH, SADHANA, SERVICE, AND JAPA

CHAPTER 24

THE STILL, SMALL VOICE OF TRUTH WITHIN

Q: Thakur, what is truth? How can we know the right path when our mind often misleads us?

Thakur was speaking to a group of devotees when someone asked this heartfelt question.

Sri Sri Bhajan Baba replied with the deepest simplicity:

"Be quiet and ask your mind. It will surely give you the answer about what is true and what is false. You will hear a response from your inner mind."

He continued,

"Even thieves, murderers, and liars—deep within—feel the knock of conscience. They may act against it, but the inner voice speaks. Most of us simply don't listen. It's easier to follow the current of worldly life than to pause and hear the still, small voice of truth within."

Thakur's message was clear: **be vigilant of your thoughts**. The scriptures call this inner voice **Vivek**—the discriminating wisdom. Those who walk the spiritual path are always advised to practice meditation and contemplation. Why? Because only in conscious awareness of one's thoughts can **self-purification** begin.

Gurudev constantly reminded us to practice *Japa* and quiet the mind, for **only in silence does purification happen**, and only in purification does one find true and lasting happiness.

CHAPTER 25

BECOMING SINCERE AND CONSISTENT IN YOUR PRACTICE

Q: Thakur, why can't I focus on the Japa mantra, even though I know that is what you want us to do—and that it is the path to peace? If I know what to do, why can't I do it?

Thakur: "Because you are not serious about your *sadhana*. You still think you can control everything and find happiness through worldly pursuits. Only when that fails do you turn to your Guru.

If you truly seek peace, then you must become sincere and consistent in your daily practice. You cannot learn anything in a single day. But if you keep doing your *Japa* with love and devotion and keep praying to your *Ishta-Guru* for divine grace, you will find that *Japa sadhana* becomes your greatest source of joy and peace."

We all make life choices based on what we believe will fulfill our deepest needs at that time. But as life unfolds—often through hardship—we begin to see the limits of ego and worldly success. It is through life's ups and downs that we awaken to the truth: the ego is not in control.

It is in these moments of collapse that a genuine longing for the divine arises. Only then does the search for the Guru and God become real. And when that inner need is true, the seeker naturally becomes serious about daily *sadhana*, seeking stability not in outer circumstances, but in inner discipline, trust, and devotion.

Over time, what seemed difficult or impossible—like focused *Japa*—becomes the very source of strength and serenity. That is the quiet miracle of spiritual life.

CHAPTER 26

PATIENCE AND PERSEVERANCE, NOT QUICK RESULTS

Q: Thakur, how long should I do Japa of the Guru Mantra to get some tangible results?

Thakur smiled and said, "That is your problem. For you, everything is about 'I do this, and I want the results right now.' But on the spiritual path, you must unlearn many things about your life. You need to empty yourself of negative habits—only then do you qualify to receive spiritual fruits. When your Japa brings you to that inner state, you will begin to feel peace and happiness—and that is the proof that you are advancing on the path of Spirit."

Thakur was pointing to a core fallacy common among spiritual seekers. Most people are conditioned from early childhood to be competitive and result-oriented in all their efforts. This mindset, while suitable for the material world, becomes an obstacle in spiritual life. According to the law of karma, any action performed with the expectation of immediate results leads to either the joy of success or the sorrow of failure.

Many enter the spiritual path carrying the same ego-driven mindset they had in the material world—a restless pursuit of instant gratification and outer recognition. But as Thakur gently reminds us, this path is not about instant coffee. It is a journey of patient perseverance, of steadily emptying the subconscious of its deeply rooted conditioning—the true source of our suffering.

Thakur emphasizes the importance of *unlearning*. Yet, most seekers try to fill their minds with excessive information from books and other sources. Ironically, this accumulation of knowledge often blocks the natural flow of spiritual energy and suppresses the unfolding of inner humility and awakened consciousness.

Thakur consistently spoke of **Japa Yoga** as a time-tested path, especially potent in this age of Kali Yuga. While it may not bring immediate results, it works silently and powerfully in the deeper layers of the subconscious, creating lasting transformation and inner bliss. The key is to stay focused on the practice, follow the guidance of the Guru, and trust the process. In due time, the seed of divinity will blossom.

CHAPTER 27

SEVA-DHARMA: THE PATH OF DIVINE SERVICE

Thakur often extolled the sacred path of *Seva-Dharma*—the way of divine service. He taught,

"Live your life in such a way that every action you perform becomes an offering—an act of worship, an act of service to the Divine. This inner attitude is the essence of all spiritual practice. There is no simpler or surer method for purifying the mind than this."

He was teaching us the art of *mindful living.* When we act with awareness, in the spirit of sacred service, even mundane tasks are transformed. They no longer generate karmic bondage but instead uplift our soul. Such awareness brings us into higher states of love, compassion, and inner joy.

Let us remind ourselves: self-centered actions driven by personal gain or pleasure can never grant lasting peace or a stress-free life. But even the simplest act, when infused with divine remembrance and selfless intention, becomes *Seva*—service to God. Such actions invoke *godliness* in the nature of the devotee. Grace flows effortlessly to those who walk the path of Karma Yoga—action steeped in love.

CHAPTER 28

REAL TAPAS IS INNER TRANSFORMATION

Q: Thakur, what is tapas—austerity or penance?

Thakur: "It is not just about physical austerities or denying yourself basic comforts or punishing the body. More than these external practices, true *tapas* is the sincere love, surrender, and deep gratitude that fills your heart for the divine grace that sustains you every moment. That inner acknowledgment of grace, that yearning for transformation—*that* is the real austerity of the heart."

People may argue about what spiritual practice works best, but the essence lies in love and devotion. Constant remembrance of the Divine, surrender to His will, and heartfelt devotion are the highest form of austerity a seeker can undertake.

Thakur strikes at the root of spiritual misunderstanding. Many seekers, unconsciously driven by ego, run after *siddhis*—miraculous powers, quick fixes, techniques to attain something extraordinary. But these very powers become the shackles of the soul. What initially pleases the ego later binds and frustrates the mind, keeping one far from divine purity.

External austerities, when performed for display or ego gratification, are empty. Thakur reminds us that *tapas* is not about the head, but the heart. It is not about showcasing renunciation, but nurturing love and devotion that leads the seeker into union with the Divine.

With deeper contemplation, it becomes clear—real *tapas* is inner transformation, born of surrender, gratitude, and love. It is the silent flame of devotion that purifies the heart and leads to the truth.

CHAPTER 29

TRUE SANNYAS IS NOT ABOUT WEARING COLORED ROBES

Q: One day, I was sitting at the feet of Thakur, and we were discussing monks from various ashrams who had been initiated into the order of Sannyas. I wanted to hear from Thakur—what, according to him, is the true meaning of Sannyas?

Thakur replied with profound depth: "*Sannyas is a state. It has nothing to do with colored robes or scriptural knowledge. You cannot 'take' sannyas. It has to manifest in you—it has to happen. When it happens, you transcend the dualistic play of intelligence and become one with the all-encompassing Consciousness.*"

It is one thing to desire renunciation and join a monastic order under the traditional Hindu system of *sannyas*—adopting ochre robes, a new name, and a new life. But what Thakur refers to is far beyond this ritualistic path. He speaks not of outward symbols, but of an inner state of realization.

True *sannyas* is the highest state of being—one who is established in the pure witnessing Self, who has gone beyond all dualities of good and evil, virtue and sin. It is the ability to perceive the same divine essence in a drain as in the sacred waters of the Ganges. It is a state beyond desire and even beyond non-desire. A state of spontaneous, wakeful being—alive in every moment, yet free from judgment or reaction.

As Thakur emphasizes, *sannyas* is not something to be adopted—it is something that blossoms, like the flowering of divinity within a human soul. It is a rare phenomenon, a manifestation of the divine that even nature takes ages to produce—a human who walks the earth yet is one with the Divine. This is *Buddhahood.* Thus, a true *sannyasi* is none other than an awakened being, a living Buddha.

CHAPTER 30

HOW TO REACH ETERNAL BLISS?

Q: Thakur, how does one attain that state of paramananda—eternal bliss?

Thakur: "Through continuous practice of *Japa*, *Dhyana*, *Bhajan*, *Kirtan*, contemplation, remembrance of the Divine, and most importantly, through the grace of Madhava (one of the Names of Lord Vishnu), you gradually ascend to that state. As you deepen your practice with love and devotion, you reach a point where your wishes are no longer separate from His. His will becomes your will. When you have no remaining desires of your own, then the bliss of Divine union dawns upon you—a bliss that is beyond cause and without condition."

Indeed, everything depends on the **intensity of your intention** to realize God or Divine wisdom in this very life. Life will always draw you into changing priorities, into the maze of worldly desires. Slowly, the mind loses its focus from meditation, prayer, and inner stillness. If this is not consciously corrected, distractions multiply, and the weight of worldly attachments pulls you away from your soul's calling. Eventually, *nirananda*—the absence of joy—creeps in, as a natural consequence of being caught in the whirlpool of desires.

But if your longing is true, and your yearning deep, if you genuinely seek freedom from the quagmire of worldliness, then a great shift occurs. You begin to remind yourself, again and again, to return to the Divine name, to dwell in the stillness of witnessing, to anchor yourself in the awareness of the Self.

Thakur is pointing toward a luminous goal: to be happy *moment to moment*, without any reason. That is **true bliss**.

CHAPTER 31

THE TRUE VALUE OF JAPA: THE MIRACLE WITHIN

Q: Thakur, you have always said we should do Japa whether we feel like it or not. But is there any real value in forced repetition if the heart isn't in it?

Thakur replied: "Yes. I have always emphasized the importance of regularity. Do your practice—whether you enjoy it or not. In the beginning, it may feel mechanical. But as you persist, the mantra becomes alive with your *prana*, your life-force. Eventually, it will become so much a part of you that even if you try, you won't be able to stop. It will be your breath, your heartbeat—your very life.

Never stop your regular practice. With time, it will become your second nature. And then, your life will be a blessing."

Most people misjudge their early struggles in spiritual practice as signs of failure. They assume that distraction or lack of enjoyment means the practice is fruitless. But **Thakur reminds us** that it is not the fleeting emotions that matter—it is **persistence, consistency, and faith**.

He often said, *"The mantra the Guru gives carries his power. When practiced with trust and perseverance, it gradually begins to cleanse the mind—inside out."*

When the focus is on **practice** rather than **instant results**, the transformation unfolds silently. Just as petals of the lotus gradually bloom within the energy centers of the body, **the hidden joy of the soul slowly awakens**.

May we all walk this path with sincerity and remember:

The miracle is not outside, but within. The Divine lives not in the sky, but in the stillness of your own heart.

All glory to Thakur, who was the **voice of conscience, the face of love, and the presence of God**—living among us in silence, simplicity, and sublime grace.

ABOUT THE AUTHOR

SHUDDHAANANDAA BRAHMACHARI (BODHI)

Shuddhaanandaa Brahmachari (Bodhi) is a globally acclaimed motivational and inspirational speaker, author, spiritual teacher, humanitarian, and peacemaker. Founder of Stress Management Academy, his Simple Art of Managing Stress and Course in Mindfulness Programs are known worldwide, inspiring corporate leadership, students, and spiritual seekers alike. His current Breath for Oneness platform offers one-on-one, family, and group virtual and in-person spiritual and life-enhancing sessions.

He is recognized as a visionary social advocate for his development of groundbreaking programs that serve thousands of poverty-stricken individuals in the slums of Kolkata, India, and remote villages of West Bengal. He founded Lokenath Divine Life Mission in 1985.

His self-authored books include: "Your Mind Your Best Friend", "Cleaning the Mirror of Mind", "Quintessence of Sai Satcharitra: A Biography of the Incredible Sai Baba of Shirdi", "The Incredible Life of a Himalayan Yogi: The Times, Teachings and Life of Living Shiva Baba Lokenath Brahmachari", "Meditations on Living Life : With Ascended Himalayan Master MahaYogi Baba Lokenath" and the inspirational biography of his Master: "Living with My Himalayan Master Sri Sri Bhajan Brahmachari—A Biography".

He was awarded the Man of Peace Award by the "World Organization for Peace in 2012 in Mexico. He has spoken at the Parliament of World Religions, United Nations Global Youth Conference, and International Conference of Spiritualizing Leadership. He received a Lifetime Achievement Award from the S.T.A.R foundation at the House of Lords in the United Kingdom on July 21, 2015, for his invaluable and outstanding contribution to society.

www.bodhiguides.com

www.ingramcontent.com/pod-product-compliance
Lightning Source LLC
Chambersburg PA
CBHW062144160726
48282CB00027B/936
* 9 7 8 8 1 9 8 2 8 6 4 3 7 *